GETTING TO KNOW THE WORLD'S GREATEST INVENTORS & SCIENTISTS

LUIS ALVAREZ

Wild Idea Man

WRITTEN AND ILLUSTRATED BY MIKE VENEZIA

CHILDREN'S PRESS®
AN IMPRINT OF SCHOLASTIC INC.
NEW YORK TORONTO LONDON AUCKLAND SYDNEY
MEXICO CITY NEW DELHI HONG KONG
DANBURY, CONNECTICUT

To Sam Venezia, one of the most inventive guys I know!

Reading Consultant: Nanci R. Vargus, Ed.D., Assistant Professor, School of Education, University of Indianapolis

Science Consultant: Doug Welch, Ph.D., Professor in the Department of Physics and Astronomy, McMaster University, Hamilton, Ontario

Photographs © 2010: Alamy Images/Steve Skjold: 12; Courtesy of American Institute of Physics, Emilio Segrè Visual Archives: 24 top (Smithsonian Museum, National Museum of American History); AP Images: 3; Corbis Images: 20, 23, 25 (Bettmann), 31 (Roger Ressmeyer); Getty Images/Time & Life Pictures: 24 bottom; Lawrence Berkeley National Laboratory Image Library: 6, 13, 15, 19, 26, 30; National Geographic Image Collection/Robert Giusti: 29; Photo Researchers, NY/David Nicholls: 22; Reuters/NASA: 7; ShutterStock, Inc./Chepe Nicoli: 18; Superstock, Inc.: 10; University of Chicago Library, Special Collections Research Center: 27.

Colorist for illustrations: Andrew Day

Library of Congress Cataloging-in-Publication Data

Venezia, Mike.
  Luis Alvarez : wild idea man / written and illustrated by Mike
Venezia.
      p. cm. — (Getting to know the world's greatest inventors and
scientists)
  Includes index.
  ISBN-13: 978-0-531-23703-8 (lib. bdg.)   978-0-531-20777-2 (pbk.)
  ISBN-10: 0-531-23703-6 (lib. bdg.)   0-531-20777-3 (pbk.)
  1. Alvarez, Luis W., 1911—Juvenile literature. 2.
Physicists—United States—Biography—Juvenile literature. I. Title.
II. Series.

  QC16.A48V46 2010
  530.092—dc22
  [B]
                         2009000356

11 12 R 19 18 17 16 15

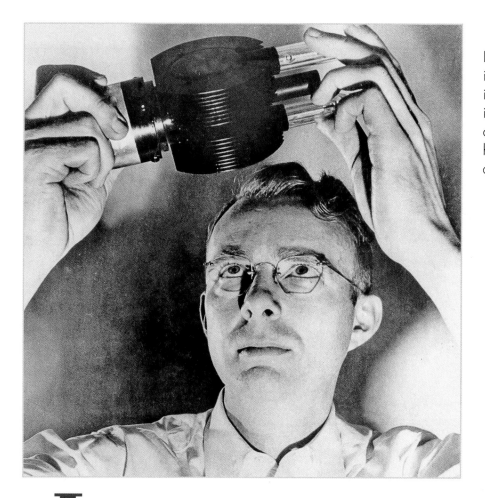

Luis Alvarez was an important physicist and inventor. Here Dr. Alvarez is shown examining a device used in a system he developed to help airplanes land in fog.

Luis Alvarez was born in San Francisco, California, in 1911. Luis, or Luie as his friends called him, grew up to become a famous experimental **physicist**. He did experiments to gather information about the universe. He also built machinery that helped unlock important secrets about the **atom**. Luis came up with so many exciting ideas that his colleagues called him the "wild idea man."

Physicists are scientists who study things like **matter,** energy, electricity, light, heat, and magnetism to see how they interact with each other. Some physicists study gigantic objects such as stars and planets. Others study atoms.

Atoms were once thought to be the smallest **particles** that make up everything in the universe. As physicists studied atoms more, they discovered that they were made up of even smaller particles. These **subatomic** particles are

so small that they can't even be seen with the
world's most powerful microscopes.

To help scientists study subatomic particles,
Luis Alvarez helped build an improved version
of a device called a **bubble chamber.** With
Luis's bubble chamber, physicists could see tiny
bubble trails that the high-energy subatomic
particles left behind. These trails gave scientists
important clues about how the mysterious
particles behaved.

In 1968, Luis Alvarez won the Nobel Prize in physics for his work on the bubble chamber. The Nobel Prize is one of the highest honors a scientist can receive.

This wasn't Luis's only important achievement, though. He was always amazing people with daring experiments and inventions.

Just after World War II began, Luis developed some new **radar** systems for the U.S. government. One of them made it possible for pilots to land their airplanes safely at night or in hazardous weather conditions. During the war, Luis helped develop the world's first **nuclear weapons.** Later in his career, Luis was asked to X-ray one of the great pyramids in Egypt to see what might be inside.

Luis Alvarez (first person on the left) and a team of scientists at Chephren's Pyramid in Egypt in 1969

This illustration shows the event that may have caused the dinosaurs to become extinct.

Luis and his geologist son also developed a theory that the extinction of the dinosaurs was caused by a gigantic **asteroid** hitting the Earth 65 million years ago.

Luis Alvarez grew up in the San Francisco area with his parents, his brother, and his two sisters. He was of Spanish-American descent. His mother had trained to be a teacher. His father was a well-known family doctor. Education was very important to the Alvarez family.

Luis didn't get to see much of his father. Dr. Alvarez spent most of his time running his practice, furthering his medical training, and doing research. Luis looked forward to any chance he might have to spend time with his father. He loved going to his dad's laboratory on Saturdays. He was fascinated with the electronic equipment his father used for medical experiments.

Luis also loved going on camping trips with his dad. On one camping trip, Luis had a close call. When he complained of stomach pains, his father was convinced Luis was having an **appendicitis** attack. Dr. Alvarez immediately prepared for an emergency operation right in the middle of the Sierra Nevada mountains! Luckily, at the last minute, Luis decided he felt better. It turned out it had just been a bad stomachache.

Moving to Minnesota, with its cold, snowy winters (above), was quite a change for Luis's family.

At the end of Luis's second year of high school, Dr. Alvarez got a terrific job offer. He was invited to work at the famous Mayo Clinic in Rochester, Minnesota. The clinic was, and still is, one of the world's leading medical-treatment and research centers. In 1926, Luis's family moved to Minnesota. It was quite a shock for them, because they had never lived in cold weather. Sometimes the temperature there would drop to 30 degrees below zero!

Once, Luis's little sister, Bernice, almost froze to death while walking home from school. She was so cold that she stopped dead in her tracks and couldn't move. Fortunately, Luis found her and was able to carry her home to safety. Even though it was a challenge getting used to the cold, Luis enjoyed his new school and made lots of friends.

Luis loved science, but he found his high-school science classes pretty boring. He was thrilled when his father got him a summer job in the Mayo Clinic machine shop. There was nothing boring about learning how to make gears and parts for medical instruments. Luis loved to work on anything mechanical. He developed skills in the machine shop that would come in handy later in his career.

Luis Alvarez studied physics at the University of Chicago (above).

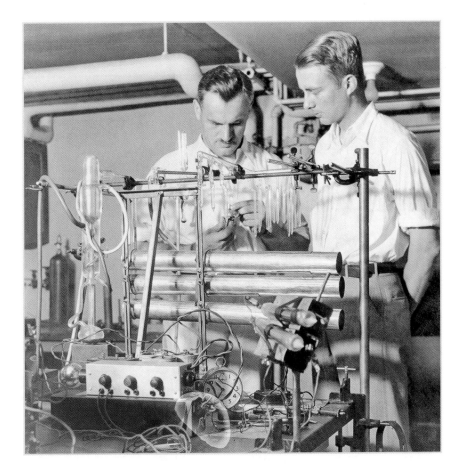

As a young graduate student at the University of Chicago, Luis Alvarez (at right) studied **cosmic rays** with renowned physicist Arthur Compton (at left). Cosmic rays are fast-moving, high-energy particles that enter the Earth's atmosphere from space.

After high school, Luis entered the University of Chicago, a school known for its excellent science programs and Nobel prize-winning professors. Luis started out majoring in chemistry. In his third year, though, he tried a class in physics.

Luis discovered that he loved physics. He enjoyed measuring light with special equipment. He couldn't wait to find out everything he possibly could about physics.

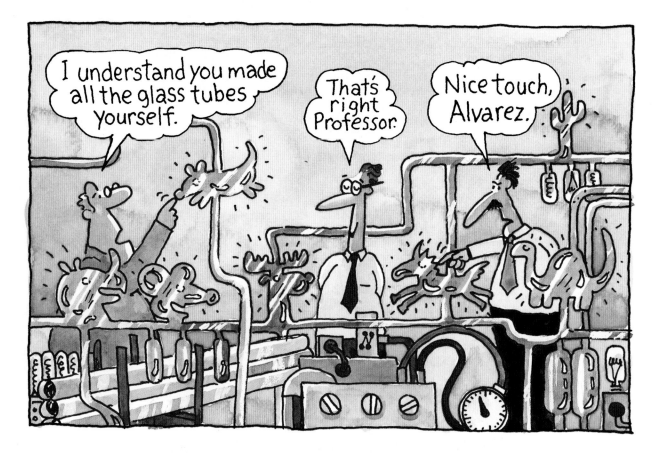

Luis Alvarez turned out to be a brilliant physics student. Once, the university needed a **Geiger counter** to measure levels of **radioactivity.** Radioactivity is the release of energy that occurs when certain atoms break apart. The physics department asked Luis to build a Geiger counter for them. This kind of instrument had just been invented in Germany. Hardly anyone knew much about it.

Luis read everything he could find to learn how a Geiger counter worked. Then he managed to build one. Luis made all the metal parts himself. He even learned glassblowing to make the tubes that were needed. Luis impressed his professors so much that they began asking him to help them find solutions to other physics problems.

This photograph shows Luis holding a scientific instrument he built a few years after he finished school.

Luis met his first wife, Geraldine Smithwick, at the University of Chicago, where she was also a student. Luis and Geri found they had a lot in common, and soon fell in love.

In 1936, Luis received his Ph.D. in physics, and he and Geri got married right away. They then left Chicago for the University of California at Berkeley, where Luis had been offered a job as a researcher. Luis and Geri would eventually have two children, Walter and Jean.

At the University of California, Luis soon began to make a name for himself as an important scientist and professor. He worked alongside some of the world's greatest physicists. One of them was Dr. Ernest Lawrence. He was famous for an invention called a **cyclotron.**

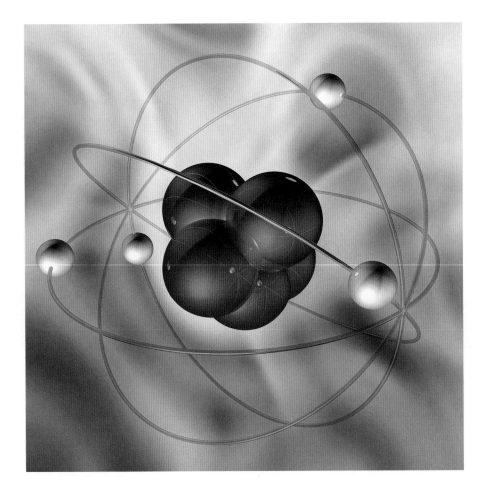

An artist's representation of an atom

In 1939, at the University of California at Berkeley, Alvarez (perched above everybody else) worked with Ernest Lawrence (third from left) and other researchers on the cyclotron.

The central part of an atom is called its **nucleus.** The cyclotron provided clues about how the atom and the parts that make up its nucleus behaved. Working with the cyclotron, Luis Alvarez made important discoveries about the energy contained in an atom's nucleus. These discoveries helped pave the way toward people being able to create **nuclear energy.**

Alvarez using a Geiger counter in the 1940s

Luis always enjoyed exchanging his ideas and discoveries with other scientists. It's one of the things that made him so successful. Every week, Luis attended gatherings at Professor Lawrence's home to see what other scientists and students had been working on.

Luis also joined the American Physical Society. This organization brought scientists together from all over the country to exchange ideas and spark each other's imaginations. Luis thought this was one of the best ways to learn about physics.

In 1939, Luis Alvarez was astonished to learn that scientists in Germany had found a way to split the tiny nucleus of an atom apart. Scientists already suspected that a nucleus could release a huge amount of energy if there were some way to chip or break it apart. But no one knew how to do it.

An artist's representation of nuclear fission

Dr. Robert Oppenheimer

Now that the new process, called **fission,** had been discovered, a whole new and exciting world was opened up to physicists. Dr. Robert Oppenheimer, a well-known professor whom Luis had worked with, made a prediction. He calculated that particles released from fission would shoot off and break apart the nucleus of other nearby atoms. Oppenheimer believed a chain reaction would begin, creating a huge amount of nuclear energy. He thought that nuclear energy could even be used to power cities someday.

The atomic bomb was first tested on July 16, 1945, over a remote area of New Mexico. Dr. Alvarez observed the explosion from an airplane and made this drawing of what he saw.

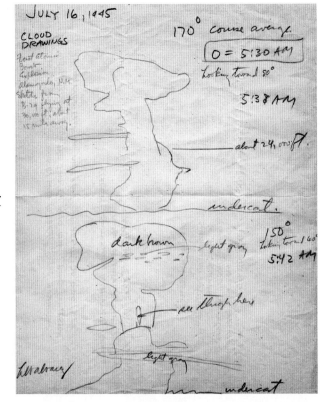

Unfortunately, nuclear energy was first used to make the most powerful bombs ever known. In 1941, the United States entered World War II. The fighting took place in Europe against Adolf Hitler and his Nazi army, and in the South Pacific against Japan. Many people believed that whoever developed an **atomic bomb** first would win the war.

On August 6, 1945, the United States dropped an atomic bomb on Hiroshima, Japan. Three days later, it dropped a second bomb (nicknamed "Fat Man" and shown at left) on Nagasaki, Japan. Luis developed the technique that was used to set off the second bomb.

In the United States, a secret project was started to make the world's first atomic bomb. Its code name was the Manhattan Project. Luis Alvarez was invited to take part in the project.

Luis and his colleagues were successful. On August 6, 1945, the first of two atom bombs was dropped over Japan. Thousands of people lost their lives on that day.

The atomic bombs dropped on Hiroshima (above) and Nagasaki caused horrible destruction and killed hundreds of thousands of people.

Dropping the atomic bombs shocked Japan into surrendering, and World War II soon ended. Even though the destruction and loss of life was horrible, Luis believed that if the war had dragged on, many more lives would have been lost on both sides.

After the war, Luis returned to his lab in Berkeley, California. He couldn't wait to get back to teaching and making new scientific discoveries. He spent the next few years discovering and experimenting with subatomic particles. He also began work on his bubble chamber.

Dr. Luis Alvarez with his liquid-hydrogen bubble chamber in 1968

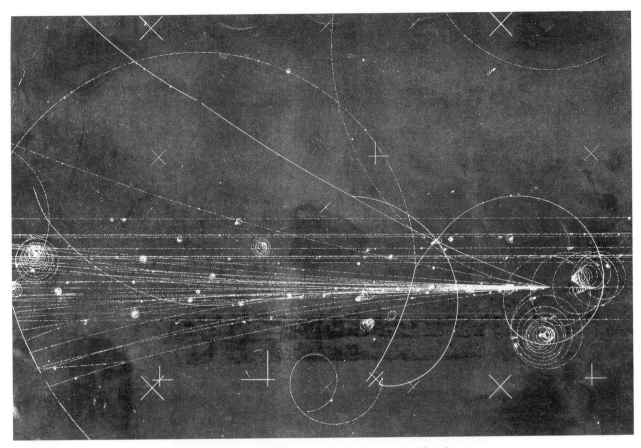

Alvarez's bubble chamber allowed scientists to record images like this one of the tiny bubble trails left behind by subatomic particles.

Luis wasn't the first person to make a bubble chamber. But he worked with other scientists to build bigger chambers that made particle bubble trails easier to see. With Luis's big bubble chambers, physicists were able to capture clearer and more detailed images of the trails in photographs. These images revealed the many interesting ways that subatomic particles can interact at high energies.

Luis Alvarez spent his whole life finding solutions to scientific problems. He was a kind of science detective. In his later years, Luis turned his attention to solving two puzzling mysteries.

The first had to do with the great pyramids in Egypt. Experts thought that one of the pyramids might contain secret, treasure-filled chambers. Luis devised a way to "X-ray" the pyramid. What he discovered was that there weren't any

Triceratops, which lived about 65 million years ago, were among the last dinosaurs to roam the Earth.

secret chambers. He wasn't upset, though. Luis was happy to have solved the mystery.

In 1980, Luis and his geologist son Walter came up with a possible answer to another mystery: why all the dinosaurs and most land animals on Earth disappeared about 65 million years ago.

Luis (left) and his son Walter (right) based their dinosaur-extinction theory on the discovery of a worldwide layer of clay (shown above) containing a mineral called iridium. They theorized that the iridium had been deposited after a huge asteroid hit Earth.

Luis and Walter found evidence that a giant asteroid must have slammed into the Earth millions of years ago. The explosion could have kicked up enough dirt, rock, and dust to fill the atmosphere and block out sunlight. After months of darkness, plants died. Over time, the dinosaurs that fed on the plants began to starve to death. Meat-eating dinosaurs died out because they no longer had prey to eat. Also, because of the lack of sunlight, the temperature probably become too cold for dinosaurs to survive.

Some scientists disagreed with the theory. They wanted to know why no one had ever found a crater big enough to have been caused by a giant asteroid. Then a few years later, a 190-mile-wide crater was discovered in Mexico. It was large enough to support Luis and Walter's theory.

Unfortunately, Luis never knew about this crater. He had died in 1988, several years before the discovery. Eventually, more and more scientists began to agree that Luis and Walter's theory was the most likely explanation for the sudden extinction of the dinosaurs.

This 1985 photograph, taken during a visit to a physics classroom, shows Walter and Luis Alvarez peering through a star dome, which shows the location of stars in relation to Earth.

Glossary

appendicitis (uh-pen-duh-SYE-tiss) An illness caused by an infected appendix

asteroid (ASS-tuh-roid) A small, rocky body that travels around the sun

atom (AT-uhm) The tiniest part of an element that has all the properties of that element

atomic bomb (uh-TOM-ik BOM) A powerful bomb, the explosion of which results from the energy released when atoms split apart

bubble chamber (BUH-buhl CHAYM-bur) A chamber of superheated liquid in which the path of an ionizing particle is made visible by a string of vapor bubbles

cosmic ray (KOZ-mik RAY) A fast-moving, high-energy particle that enters the Earth's atmosphere from space

cyclotron (SIKE-luh-tron) A device used to create high-energy nuclear particles by bouncing them off each other at high speeds

fission (FISH-uhn) In physics, the splitting of the nucleus of an atom, resulting in the release of large amounts of energy

Geiger counter (GYE-gur KOUN-tur) A device that finds and measures radioactivity

matter (MAT-ur) Anything that has weight and takes up space

nuclear energy (NOO-klee-ur EN-uhr-jee) Energy created by splitting atoms

nuclear weapon (NOO-klee-ur WEP-uhn) A weapon that uses the power created by splitting atoms

nucleus (NOO-klee-uhss) The central part of an atom

particle (PAR-tuh-kuhlz) In physics, a minute part of an atom

physicist (FIZ-ih-sist) A scientist in the field of physics, the science that deals with matter and energy

radar (RAY-dar) A device that sends out radio waves and picks them up again after the waves strike an object and bounce back

radioactivity (ray-dee-oh-ack-TIV-ih-tee) The release of energy that occurs when the central parts of certain atoms break apart

subatomic (sub-uh-TOM-ik) Smaller than or occurring within an atom

Index